D1398232

Print Uppercase and Lowercase Letters, Words, and Silly Phrases

Kindergarten and First Grade Writing Practice Workbook (Reproducible)

by Julie Harper

/

Print Uppercase and Lowercase Letters, Words, and Silly Phrases: Kindergarten and First Grade Writing Practice Workbook (Reproducible)

Children's Books > Education & Reference > Words & Language

Children's Books > Education & Reference > Education > Workbooks

ISBN 10: 1479175455

EAN 13: 978-1479175451

Table of Contents

Introduction 4
Uppercase Alphabet 5
Lowercase Alphabet 6
Part 1 Trace and Copy Uppercase and Lowercase Letters 7
Part 2 Trace and Copy Silly Words and Phrases 59

Introduction

The goal of this unique writing workbook is to engage children and motivate learning through the use of creativity. Children enjoy reading silly words like "rhinophant" and "banana taco." Exercises like these help to make learning fun, whether in the classroom or at home.

This Print Wacky Sentences writing workbook focuses on writing uppercase and lowercase letters, words, and short phrases.

Two sections of this workbook help students develop their writing skills at different levels:
- ✓ In Part 1, students practice tracing and copying uppercase and lowercase letters. The three traditional horizontal lines are included as a guide – solid top and bottom lines plus a dashed middle line help students master the relative heights of the letters, and to write across the page in straight lines.
- ✓ Part 2 advances onto writing silly words or phrases, like "banana taco."

May your students or children improve their writing skills and enjoy reading and writing these silly words.

Uppercase Alphabet

Lowercase Alphabet

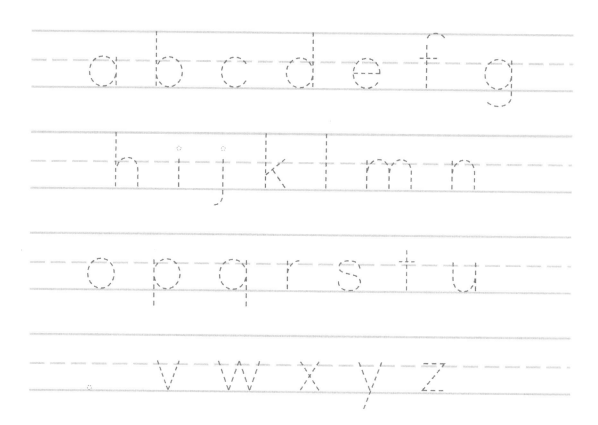

Part 1 Trace and Copy Uppercase and Lowercase Letters

Part 1 Instructions: Trace directly over these dotted letters. Then write the letters on your own on the following (blank) line.

B B B B B B B B

B B B B B B B B

b b b b b b b b

b b b b b b b b

B B B B B B B B

B B B B B B B B

b b b b b b b b

b b b b b b b

E E E E E E E E E E

E E E E E E E E E E

e e e e e e e e

e e e e e e e e

P P P P P P P P

P P P P P P P

p p p p p p p

p p p p p p p

P P P P P P P

P P P P P P P

p p p p p p p

p p p p p p p

Part 2 Trace and Copy Silly Words and Phrases

Part 2 Instructions: Trace directly over these dotted letters. Then write the words on your own on the following (blank) line.

RHINOPHANT

rhinophant

ZEBRAFFE

zebraffe

CROCOGATOR

crocogator

OCTOPANDA

octopanda

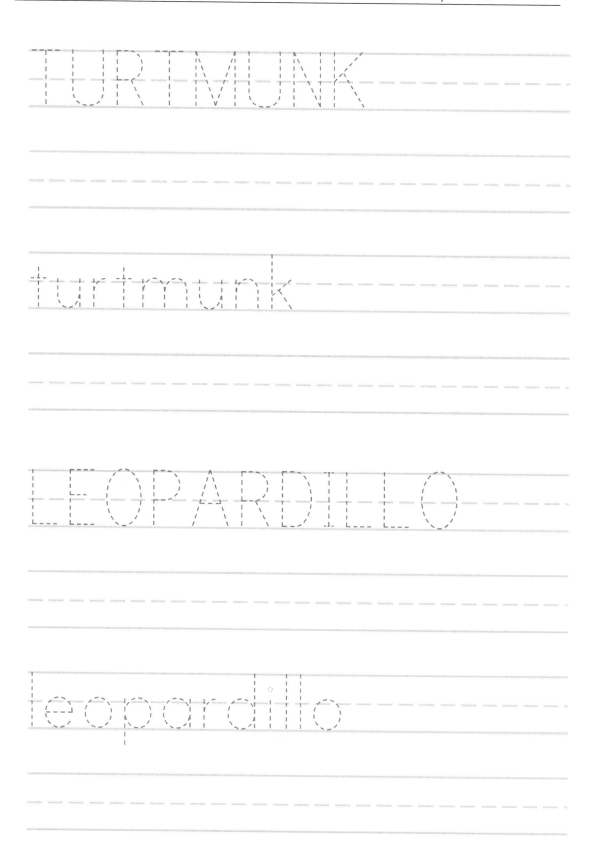

TURTMUNK

turtmunk

LEOPARDILLO

leopardillo

IGUANZEE

iguanzee

CHEETOPOTAMUS

cheetopotamus

JAGOAT

jagoat

KOALION

koalion

MONKILLA

monkilla

ORANGUVARK

oranguvark

PEACOBRA

peacobra

PENGUIPINE

penguipine

QUICK TURTLE

quick turtle

BALD MONKEY

bald monkey

SHORT GIRAFFE

short giraffe

FURRY SNAKE

furry snake

THIN HIPPO

thin hippo

FAST SNAIL

fast snail

CLEAN PIG

clean pig

QUIET PARROT

quiet parrot

TALL DASCHUND

tall daschund

TINY WHALE

tiny whale

PLAIN ZEBRA

plain zebra

GIANT ANT

giant ant

HAIRLESS APE

hairless ape

SLOW CHEETAH

slow cheetah

SHY MOSQUITO

shy mosquito

WEE ELEPHANT

wee elephant

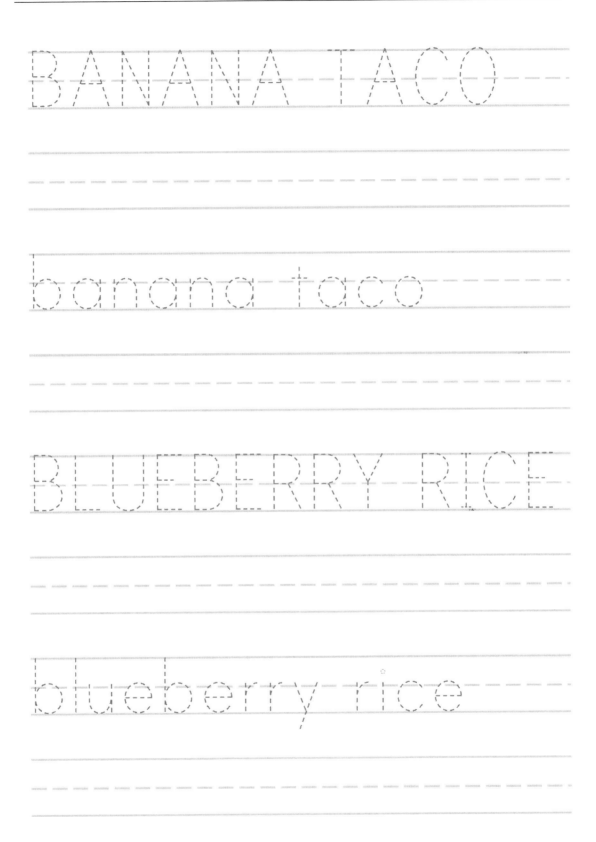

BANANA TACO

banana taco

BLUEBERRY RICE

blueberry rice

CANDY BURGER

candy burger

PLUM SPAGHETTI

plum spaghetti

CHERRY PIZZA

cherry pizza

CHOCOLATE TEA

chocolate tea

COOKIE SOUP

cookie soup

CUPCAKE BEANS

cupcake beans

GRAPE NOODLES

grape noodles

SUGAR BURRITO

sugar burrito

MELON EGGROLL

melon eggroll

MUFFIN TAMALE

muffin tamale

PEACH STIR FRY

peach stir fry

BLUE SALAD

blue salad

POPCORN FRIES

popcorn fries

VANILLA PEAS

vanilla peas

YOGURT CORN

yogurt corn

HOT DOG MILK

hot dog milk

GUMDROP EGGS

gumdrop eggs

CHEESE FUDGE

cheese fudge

EEL SNOUT COLA

eel snout cola

SNAKE LEG SOUP

snake leg soup

FISH ARM DROPS

fish arm drops

CAT BEAK JUICE

cat beak juice

BUTTERED FUR

buttered fur

BEAR FIN TOAST

bear fin toast

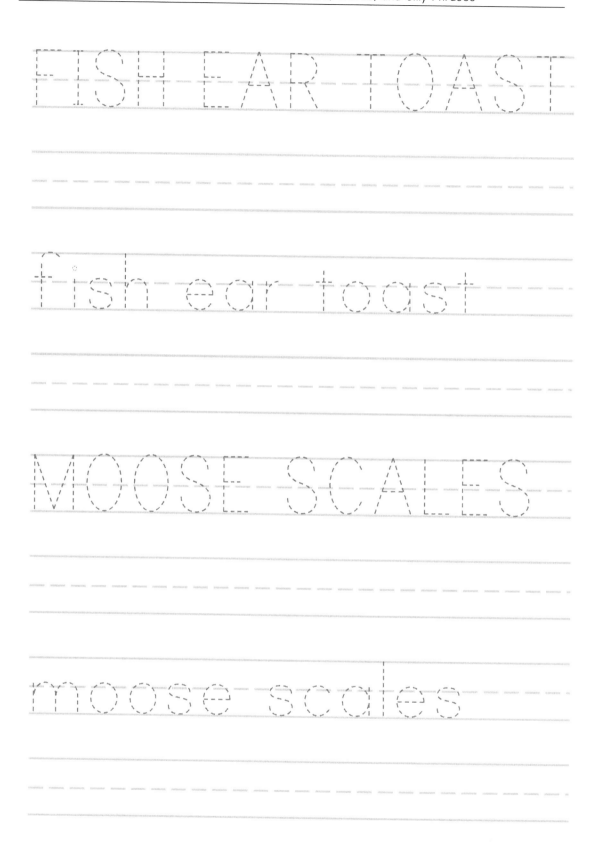

FISH EAR TOAST

fish ear toast

MOOSE SCALES

moose scales

CAT BISCUITS

cat biscuits

BUG EYE SHAKE

bug eye shake

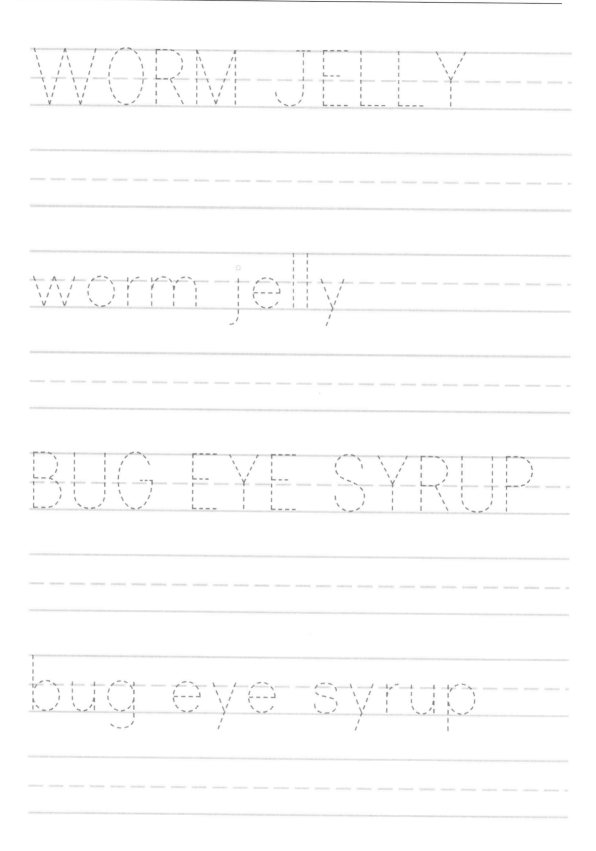

WORM JELLY

worm jelly

BUG EYE SYRUP

bug eye syrup

GOAT PANCAKES

goat pancakes

FRIED BUGERS

fried bugers

Workbooks by Julie Harper

✓ *Letters, Words, and Silly Phrases Handwriting Workbook (Reproducible): Practice Writing in Cursive (Second and Third Grade).*

✓ *Wacky Sentences Handwriting Workbook (Reproducible): Practice Writing in Cursive (Third and Fourth Grade).*

✓ Print Uppercase and Lowercase Letters, Words, and Silly Phrases: Kindergarten and First Grade Writing Practice Workbook (Reproducible).

✓ Print Wacky Sentences: First and Second Grade Writing Practice Workbook (Reproducible).

Made in the USA
Middletown, DE
23 January 2015